What others are saying
WHERE HAVE ALL THE SMAR

MW01044511

Where Have All the Smart Women Gone? underscores the need for women to believe in themselves in order to "let their light shine." A highly readable book with experiences familiar to many women.

Bev Forbes, Ed.D., Seattle University

Where Have All the Smart Women Gone? is a compelling and thought-provoking book. Written with feeling and conviction, this book encourages women to celebrate, rather than hide, their gifts and talents.

Mary Ann Swenson, Bishop, United Methodist Church, Denver Region

Bravo Alice! You've captured all that happens to the best and brightest, and in fact, all women. *Where Have All the Smart Women Gone?* belongs in every college women's center and in women's studies classes.

Laura Misencik, Director, Women's Center, Everett Community College

Where Have all the Smart Women Gone? is a thoughtful and enlightening book. As a woman, an educator, and a parent, I recommend this book be read in college courses, in women's groups, and in families.

Dr. Elizabeth Douvan, Emeritus, University of Michigan
Faculty, The Fielding Institute

As a therapist, pastor and mother, I am excited by Alice Rowe's research and writings about women's achievement. *Where Have All the Smart Women Gone?* will be a practical and inspiring resource for my clients as well as my own gifted daughters.

Penelope Guntermann, M.Div., M.A.

After reading your book, I was able to tell my husband that I am a gifted woman and that this book speaks volumes to me and validates some of my thoughts. My husband read the book, too, and said it gave him a new perspective. Your book told me it is okay to not be all things at once, and that by being just one of those doesn't make me any less smart.

Donna Foss, mother, Marysville, WA

Your book spoke so directly to my heart that I'm hard-pressed to express how much....Today I see I have a mission—to let my light shine—and your encouragement comes at yet another perfect moment.

Diana York Blaine, Ph.D., professor, Women's Studies, University of Southern California

Alice Rowe is a leader. *Where Have All the Smart Women Gone?* shows women how to surmount cultural obstacles to self-realization. Alice's counsel empowers every smart woman to achieve goals and fulfill dreams. This will be a valuable resource for our library patrons.

Betsy Lewis, Managing Librarian

As I turned each page, as I read each chapter, I saw myself reflected there. It was as if you were talking to me personally. The workbook format, with questions at the end of each chapter, caused me to pause and take a look inward, at who I am, how I've adapted, and what motivates me. You have pulled the blinds on years of dark frustration and changed the way I see myself....*Where Have All the Smart Women Gone?* should be required reading for women returning to or entering college after a prolonged absence. More importantly, I think it should be recommended to any woman who has been subjected to emotional abuse; any woman who has been told she's not smart enough to keep the family finances or adequately raise her children.

Mary Smith, parent, business analyst, graduate student, writer, Everett, Washington

WHERE HAVE ALL THE SMART WOMEN GONE?

ALICE ANN ROWE, PH.D.

Library of Congress Cataloging-in-Publication Data

Rowe, Alice Ann.
      Where have all the smart women gone? / Alice Ann Rowe
      p.cm.
      Includes bibliographical references.
      LCCN 00-108253
      ISBN -9703089-0-6

      1. Gifted women. 2. Self-actualization (Psychology)
      3. Achievement motivation in women. 4. Success.
      I Title
      BF723.G52R69 2001   155.6'33'0879
                  QBI00-901540

Smart People Books
149 Sudden Valley
Bellingham, WA 98226
fax: 360-650-1031
email: SPBooks@premier1.net

ATTENTION COLLEGES, CORPORATIONS, AND PROFESSIONAL ORGANIZATIONS.
Quantity discounts are available on bulk purchases of this book for educational, business, or sales use.
Contact Smart People Books.

To my daughter Sierra

may your light
always shine brightly

CONTENTS

A COUNTRY CALLED DOUBLE BIND

A COUNTRY CALLED CELEBRATION

FOREWORD

Recently I lunched with a new acquaintance who expressed great surprise at my accomplishments. "A Ph.D. <u>and</u> a triathlete? What's up with that?" Another friend laughed and said, "Yes, is she an overachiever or what?" Quickly I was flooded with a series of familiar emotions: shame at being pointed out for succeeding; disbelief that I was in fact a success; resentment at being called an overachiever.

I can't really say which feeling was the strongest, but I do understand that my reactions, far from being idiosyncratic, epitomize a dilemma particular to what Alice Rowe terms the "smart woman." In this book, she explores rich and unexamined territory, investigating what it means to be intelligent and female in a world that continues to value women for our capacity to please men over our value to please ourselves.

In the early nineteenth century, an increasingly capitalist United States began reformulating gender roles, matching the growing need for aggressive male workers in the public sphere by calling for docile and moral females at home. Women who rebelled against this Victorian doctrine of the separate spheres were derided as harridans bent on bringing down the entire republic by refusing to create a loving domestic environment to offset an uncharitable, unchristian marketplace.

Strong women and smart men have been battling against these stereotypes ever since. Elizabeth Cady Stanton's father gave her the education that Victorian gender constructions would have denied her; she used this opportunity to become one of our most powerful voices in the struggle for liberation, joining with Susan B. Anthony in a decades-long crusade for emancipation. Her final and most powerful speech, "The Solitude of Self," detailed the profound need for women to develop core identities and become individuals rather than always to be defined in relation to men.

Stanton's religious and political ideas were too srong for her time, even for many women who joined her in the march for suffrage, and she has lapsed into an obscurity that threatens to preclude women of the following centuries from building on her powerful example. While many of the reforms she and her feminist sisters fought for have come to fruition, the fundamental right for women to be people--brilliant people--still chafes against more prevailing notions that only men should shine so brightly.

While Title Nine legislation slowly becomes implemented, and we finally equip our little girls with access to athletics, we have yet to equip them with the permission to be truly individual. Advertisements bombard them with images of female perfection, which today idealizes near anorexic physical weakness and dictatcs that they should constantly maneuver for male attention and approval. The Spice Girls, Britney Spears, and a host of other sexist role models guarantee that another generation of women will be anxious about their bodies. Brainy girls, I fear, will still wish instead for beauty, as I, and my mother before me, did.

Now, thanks to the work our foremothers did, we have been given the opportunity to educate ourselves. But can we resist the debilitating cultural messages in order to fully embrace the dazzling achievements of which we are all so capable? And can we even know how to define success for ourselves? Men have traditionally been asked to sacrifice intimacy in order to climb the corporate ladder. Must we give up close relationships if we, too, seek material success?

I find as a Professor of Women's Studies that the answers to these questions lie in dialogue with smart women and the smart girls that we mentor. Alice Rowe's book comes as a crucial voice in this conversation, an opportunity to interrupt the mainstream demands for our mental submission, our physical alteration, our emotional dependence. Mothers need to read this book with their daughters; women need to share these ideas with their friends. Husbands, fathers and brothers, too, need to be made aware of the stuggle that we have in viewing ourselves as people, not help-mates, dolls, or bitches.

This work first came to my attention as I was struggling to find my voice in a male-dominated academy that would have my visionary ideas silenced. Rowe's work helped make clear to me my ambivalence about disrupting male "truths," my confusion over what a female professor looks and sounds like, my difficulty in constructing a healthy sense of self. I am only too happy to participate in this book so that I may say, five years later, I have grown stronger, physically and mentally, no longer looking to a sexist culture for self definition, yes, Ph.D., and triathlete. Today, even as many students, colleagues, and friends still resist my call for women to be fully human, I am proud to be a smart woman who will not go away.

Diana York Blaine
University of Southern California

INTRODUCTION

"I can ride a horse, I know," said Sarah. "I rode once when I was twelve. I will ride Jack." Jack was Sarah's favorite. Papa shook his head. "Not Jack," he said. "Jack is sly." "I am sly, too," said Sarah stubbornly.
—Patricia MacLachlan, *Sarah, Plain and Tall*

In writing this book, my mission is to encourage you to celebrate your gifts and talents. Don't hide them, and don't let yourself be talked out of them. Instead, let your light shine.

I'd like to explain how I came to write this book. Its source is my doctoral dissertation, "Let Our Light Shine: Women and Childhood Giftedness." I have always had a strong interest in the subject of women and their achievements. When I was a young girl, my parents let me know that I could achieve whatever I wanted. "The world is open to you," they told me.

My interest in the subject of women and achievement began in earnest at Simmons College, a New England private women's college, which was dedicated to preparing women for careers. All around me, campus leaders were women. In addition, the feminist movement was a formative part of my 20's and 30's, so equality for women is still an important issue for me. As I entered the workplace, I watched how women moved up in the organization...or did not. In graduate school and since, I have read profusely about women's development. When I had a son and a daughter, I wanted both of them to grow up seeing women as capable as men, each gender with its strengths and weaknesses.

While I was working on my doctorate, our daughter, Sierra, was placed in a gifted program in her school district in Anacortes, Washington. In this program, the children stayed in the same classroom together, Monday through Friday, all year long. In this way, she was surrounded by other children who were also highly capable.

Even though I felt gifted programs were a good idea, I needed to learn more about them. I began reading as much as I could about children and giftedness. I wondered what the long-term effects would be for Sierra. Ultimately, would it help or hurt her to be set apart as "gifted?" Wasn't everyone gifted in some way? When Sierra grew up, would she look back on her time in that gifted program and say that it was good for her life?

Rather than wait for Sierra to grow up, I studied college-educated women between the ages of thirty and fifty, who had been placed in gifted programs by their school systems. I met with them in focus groups of five to seven women. I asked each group the same questions, and tape-recorded those conversations. Then I transcribed those conversations, and as I read them over and over, clear themes began to emerge from one group to another. It is these conversations that were the basis for my doctoral dissertation and for this book. Most of the quotes you will read come from those thirty-four women who shared deeply about their lives. I am grateful to them for their time and their reflections.

I want to emphasize that this book is not just for women who, as students, were set apart as "gifted." It's true that the study I conducted was about gifted women. But I believe the themes in their lives overlap with those of all women, whether or not they are seen by others as gifted. You will find themes in this book that connect to your own life.

The women in my study spoke of giftedness in broad terms, not just in terms of brightness or ability to do well in school. According to one researcher, the definition of giftedness in women needs to include

the nurturance of one's children and family, the success of being an outstanding teacher, and the joy of accomplishment from the pursuit of a career that still allows time for a satisfying personal life....The way we view female "giftedness" may have to be expanded beyond an assessment of women's professional accomplishments.
—*Sally Reis,* Gifted Child Quarterly

The women in my study balanced their own high achievements with their personal success in finding "what really matters in life."

In the chapters that follow, I will tell you about themes in women's lives discovered through my research. First, I'll examine some of the themes that *discourage* us from "letting our light shine." This section in the book is entitled "A Country Called Double Bind." Second, I'll look at the themes that *encourage* us, plus steps we can take to arrive at what I describe as "A Country Called Celebration."

This book gives you an opportunity to reflect, write, and encourage others. As you read each theme, think about how it relates to your own life. You can journey through it on your own, answering the questions at the end of each chapter. Or you can make this journey with those of similar interests. As a mother, you can journey with your daughter, talking and writing about generational differences together. Or, you can travel through the pages with other women friends, meeting in a weekly study group. Whatever you do, I invite you to explore it with an open mind and open heart.

Women in the Study
in alphabetical order (names have been changed)

Name	Profession	Name	Profession
Anne	nurse	Kelly	lawyer
Betty	nurse	Liz	teacher
Brenda	teacher	Lynn	teacher
Carly	doctor	Martha	teacher
Diana	nurse	Mary	financial agent
Elaine	manager	Penny	teacher & writer
Hope	teacher	Rachel	teacher
Jenny	teacher of gifted children	Rose	teacher of gifted children
Jill	teacher	Roxanne	manager
Joan	doctoral student	Ruth	nurse
Joy	manager	Shelly	manager
June	engineer	Sue	engineer

STEP OUT OF
THE BEATEN PATH

I honor every woman who has strength enough to step out of the beaten path when she feels that her walk lies in another; strength enough to stand up and be laughed at, if necessary. But in a few years it will not be thought strange that women should be preachers and sculptors, and every one who comes after us will have to bear fewer and fewer blows.

—Harriet Hosmer in *Daughters of America*, 1883

I strongly believe in our abilities and worth as women. We can overcome conditions that limit our life choices. Unfortunately, we tend to downplay our visions, dreams, gifts, and talents. Why is it so hard for us to believe that we are as competent as we truly are? What's the big deal? Two things are a "big deal:" one is history, and another is culture.

Historical views of women

Throughout history, experts in medicine and education have viewed women's intellectual abilities as limited, at best. To these experts, women and intelligence were clearly a contradiction in terms. The phrase "smart woman" was an oxymoron. To give you an idea of what I mean, consider the following comments by famous thinkers:

Women's entire education should be planned in relation to men. To please men, to be useful to them, to win their love and respect, to raise them as children, care for them as adults, counsel and console them, make their lives sweet and pleasant.
—Jean-Jacques Rousseau (1712-1778)

When a woman inclines to learning, there is usually something wrong with her sex apparatus.
—Friedrich Nietzsche (1844-1900)

No dress or garment is less becoming to a woman than a show of intelligence.
—Martin Luther (1483-1546)

A woman who has a head full of Greek, or carries on fundamental controversies about mechanics, might as well have a beard.
—Immanuel Kant (1724-1804)

In 1879, a psychologist by the name of Le Bon expressed this chilling view of women:

All psychologists who have studied the intelligence of women, as well as poets and novelists, recognize today that they represent the most inferior forms of human evolution and that they are closer to children and savages than to an adult, civilized male. Without doubt there exist some distinguished women, very superior to the average man, but they are as exceptional as the birth of any monstrosity, as, for example, of a gorilla with two heads.

Besides Le Bon, other leading psychologists of the nineteenth century claimed that women were inferior, not only in brains but in character:

• G. Stanley Paul (1844-1924), an educator as well as a renowned psychologist, recommended that education for women should center around preparing them for motherhood.
• Sigmund Freud (1856-1939) described the main traits of femininity as narcissism, masochism, and passivity.
• Carl Jung (1875-1961) noted the mentally healthy female as being more emotional and less rational and logical than an equally mentally healthy male.

In 1873, Dr. Edward Clark, a Boston physician and formerly of the Harvard Medical School, warned that women could ruin their health if they attempted to study college subjects. The reason for this, he contended, was that it takes all of a woman's strength and resources to get her reproductive system in proper order!

These views both reflected and reinforced the prevailing social attitudes of the day. No wonder self image has long been a problem for women! We need new words—new quotations—that reflect women as fully capable and intelligent people.

Cultural views of women

The second "big deal" is culture. Smart, educated women have not been fully affirmed by our culture. Anything more than a grade-school education was virtually denied to American women until the late nineteenth century. Until then, women could not gain entry to most universities or careers.

At that point, women like Susan B. Anthony and Dorothy Day challenged society's norms. Though they were scorned repeatedly, they gradually gained wide support for changes in education and politics. Today we have easier entry into colleges and careers because of pioneers like them.

Both the suffragette movement and the more recent women's movement have contributed to a growing perception of women as smart, capable individuals. But we still don't hear from our culture a strong enough message to use our gifts and abilities. Instead we hear conflicting messages: "It's best for you to stay home with the kids, dear, but I also want you to get a job to pay some bills around here." Or, "As a junior executive in this company, feel free to offer suggestions, but leave the major decisions to the men in the boardroom." In addition, there is much conflict between the value we place on the role of mothers at home and the expectation that "of course" motivated, competent women will want to be in the workplace. Though in many ways women have taken their place along with men in the workplace, I look forward to the day when *men* will worry about how to combine career and family!

More than anything else, women are given the message that it is better to have a life of security and dependence rather than a life of risk and independence. But this message is not consistent with today's realities.

• • • • •

What do you see as three of your strongest gifts and talents? Do you feel you are celebrating those gifts and talents now? What keeps you from celebrating them more fully? What is your main roadblock? Who is your strongest encourager?

NOTES

NOTES

A COUNTRY CALLED DOUBLE BIND

2

LAND OF LOST DREAMS:
"You can do anything (but that)."

"Didn't anyone ever tell you it was all right to write?" asked the psychiatrist. "Yes, but not to be a writer." Behind me lay the sort of middle-class education that encourages writing, painting, music, theater, so long as they aren't taken too seriously, so long as they can be set aside once the real business of life begins."

—*Jane Cooper,* Maps and Windows

Where did all the smart women go? They emigrated to a country I call Double Bind. This is not a literal country, but it is a place that many of us understand on a deep level, because we have been there ourselves. The country of Double Bind is a symbol for the dilemmas that women find themselves in, if they happen to be bright as well as competent. As they strive to achieve professional success and recognition, they still feel societal pressure to assume more conventional roles. This country contains four lands: Lost Dreams, Sexism, Dumbing Down, and No Cracks Allowed.

Nearly half the women in my study said that as young girls, they believed they could achieve anything. The following comments from eight different women are typical of a theme repeated throughout the study:

I had the sense from grade school, when I first knew I was bright, that I could do anything and be anything that I wanted to be, and I never lost that completely. (Rose)

I was taught I could do anything I wanted to do, but I don't know how I was taught that. I guess I presumed I could do whatever I wanted to do. (Anne)

I can't remember anybody ever telling me there wasn't anything I couldn't do. What ever I wanted to do, I could do it. (Sue)

I felt like there wasn't anything I couldn't do. Everything was out there. (Roxanne)

Some women in the group still feel invincible today:

I have this inner confidence that I can do whatever I want to do, and I can do it really well. (Liz)

I feel like there are solutions to every single problem. (Lynn)

Now my problem for me is to decide what I want to do, because I've realized that I can do anything that I want to do. (Elaine)

I'm used to winning. (Shelly)

With such a strong message to reach for the stars, did the women in my study go on to accomplish great things? In school, yes. In the confines of the classroom, they were given license to achieve. It was appropriate to excel.

Even though gifted girls often receive excellent grades, however, it doesn't necessarily follow that they will achieve their own high goals when they graduate. One reason for this ironic twist: they face a double bind. During school they were told, "You can do anything." But outside of the classroom, they are often given a different message from well-meaning friends, relatives and employers: "But of course, you can't do <u>that</u>."

Even when the gifted female student is encouraged to study in the field of her choice, the message she receives as an adult is that her success is measured as a wife and mother, not as a professional. If she succeeds in all three roles, critics nevertheless insist that she must be doing a poor job in one of them.

—*Linda Schwartz*, Gifted Child Quarterly

When they were young, the women in my study heard the message that they <u>could</u> do anything, but they weren't necessarily offered the skills to <u>do</u> it. Along the way, some women lost their dreams, letting go of their career goals.

A majority of the women in my study admitted feeling guilty they were not making full use of the gifts they had been given. One member spoke for the group when she said, "I feel as though there are some things that I'm supposed to do, and I'm trying to figure out what they are."

Some felt they should be accomplishing great, earth-shattering feats at this time in their lives. Brenda, a teacher in the group, had dreamed of becoming an atomic scientist, but that dream was discouraged by her husband:

I was going to be an atomic scientist, and I had a scholarship to go to Oak Ridge to study. Then I met my husband-to-be, and when I told him at a dance what my plans were, he pushed me away, and it was really hard. He said, 'Is there anything else that you've thought about being?' I said, 'Yes, a teacher.' He pulled me back in, and we talked about that. That's what I became.

It's interesting to note that three women who aspired to be doctors are currently teachers, a profession that nurtures and supports rather than performs.

One of these women, Rose, said she had dreamed of becoming a medical doctor or getting a Ph.D. "I was going to change the world," she smiled, "and I was going to be a medical missionary to Africa on the side." Instead, she rebelled against her parents' high expectations at 18 and married a logger. That marriage ended in divorce.

A second teacher, Martha, lost her dream of being a doctor when her I-can-do-anything bubble burst unexpectedly, when she "crashed and burned" as soon as she entered college:

I was on academic probation my first semester of college. I was going to be able to do anything. I just simply abandoned that [becoming a doctor] completely after struggling in math and science.

Another teacher in my study had seriously considered going to medical school, adding that friends encouraged her to do so, but her parents were strongly opposed to it, so she backed down.

One woman in the group who *did* become a doctor feels, ironically, she lost her dream of becoming an artist. "There was so much pressure in school and home to achieve," she explained, "that my artistic self didn't have a chance to develop."

Happily, the other physician in the group felt she had attained the high career goal she set for herself when she was young. Said Carly, "I knew since fifth grade that I was going to be a doctor." In this study, though, her fulfillment of a childhood goal was more the exception than the rule.

Why weren't these dreams fulfilled? Besides a strong message of discouragement from others, one reason seemed to be the lack of female role models in certain fields. Ruth, a nurse, said:

> *Whatever I did, I did well, but if I had to point to something that kept me from trying out a different career, I think it would be the lack of female role models. I didn't see in front of me what the possibilities were.* (emphasis added)

Anne, also a nurse, could not picture herself in the career she had in mind originally, partly because she saw no women entering that field:

> *I wanted to be a nuclear engineer when I started high school, but I couldn't see myself doing that. I couldn't imagine myself in a tie and wing-tipped shoes.*

Many in the focus group wondered aloud what they would have become, had more choices been offered to them. Lack of parents' encouragement was a big factor in staying with "safer" choices. Said Ruth:

> *There may have been something to my parents not pushing me to be a doctor. If they had, maybe I would have been one.*

Reflected two others, currently teachers:

> *I thought a lot about [being a doctor], but there were so few female role models.*

Maybe I could have persevered and done the doctor thing. Clearly I could have done that, but in terms of where my heart really lives, which is writing, I didn't know anybody like that. So I did the teacher thing. Fortunately, I'm in a program that keeps me stimulated, but I'm really bored with most of it. What should I do next? I don't know. (Jenny)

Sometimes I wish I had known about more opportunities to broaden my horizons. Growing up in a rural Midwestern community, I remember the first time I saw a public library. I thought, "Oh, I want to read every book." There was so much I didn't know about.   I think of all [that's contained] in already-made choices. (Rose)

Often when I am invited to speak at conferences, I emphasize how important it is to give messages of support and encouragement to the young women in our lives. We need to teach them they have many choices and don't have to choose *only one* profession. The question we need to ask them is not, "What do you want to do?" but rather, "What do you want to do *first?*"

• • • • •

Have you travelled to this land of "Lost Dreams"? What did you want to be when you grew up? What did you tend to do when people discouraged you from reaching for the stars? What did you do when people encouraged your dreams? Have you achieved one or more of those career dreams? What do you want to accomplish now? (For a related chapter covering the positive side of this theme, see "Land of Achieving: Dreams Regained")

NOTES

N O T E S

3

LAND OF SEXISM:
"Yes, you're bright, but shut up."

The best advice I can give you is to stop writing and go back to the South and have some babies. The greatest woman is not the woman who has written the finest book but the woman who has had the finest babies.
—a literary man, in a letter to Ellen Glasgow, writer

In addition to a lack of female role models, a related reason for not achieving one's dreams is cultural sexism. That is the second land in this country called Double Bind.

In various ways, both subtle and direct, our culture discourages women from expressing their intelligence. Nearly all studies about gifted women touch on this theme. In Tillie Olsen's *Silences*, a book chiding society for its suppression of artists, she mentions gifted women in particular:

Where the gifted among women...have remained mute, or have never attained full capacity, it is because of circumstances, inner and outer, which oppose the needs of creation.

What are these circumstances that "oppose the needs of creation" by gifted women, in particular? Harvard psychologist Carol Gilligan studied and worked with young girls.

Around the age of eleven, she discovered, girls go through a "moment of resistance"—a clarity of vision, a high sense of confidence in what they know and see, and a belief in their own integrity. "Eleven-year olds are not for sale," wrote Gilligan.

But during adolescence, there comes a crisis of confidence. Gilligan believes the strictures of our culture send a particular message to women: "Keep quiet; notice the absence of women [in power], and say nothing."

> *At Iowa, a classmate told me he believed that to be a woman poet was "a contradiction in terms." Princeton intensified my own sense of dichotomy between "woman" and "poet." I knew a number of men who wrote, but no women.*
> —*Jane Cooper*, Maps and Windows

By age fifteen or sixteen, that resistance has gone underground. "They start saying, 'I don't know.' They start not knowing what they had known." Gilligan and her associates were dismayed at repeatedly seeing "a morally articulate preadolescent transformed into an apologetic, hesitant teenager."

This profound change occurs when adolescent girls come up against the wall of Western culture. Gilligan found that the girls would "begin to see that their clear-sightedness may be dangerous and seditious. They learn to hide and protect what they know—not only to censor themselves but 'to think in ways that differ from what they really think.'" Gilligan called this "going underground."

Gilligan and her colleagues have been looking for ways to strengthen healthy resistance and courage in girls, so they can avoid doubting what they know. We need to know much more about how to nurture and encourage gifted girls.

Research by a psychologist who studied with Gilligan had similar findings. Emily Hancock concluded, "A female easily loses sight of who she really is, beneath the feminine facade she adopts in youth." As an elementary student, a young girl is often encouraged in her giftedness—until the culture begins to define her as female instead of a person. By preadolescence and adolescence, "along comes the culture with the pruning shears, ruthlessly trimming back her spirit. Myriad ways are found to pinch the girl back and shape her."

Many women in Hancock's study found that "cultural expectations of females had led them to displace the essence of who and what they were." These expectations divide a girl against herself, "driving the essential girl to an inner realm where she remains hidden—even from herself." Often a false self steals in to take the girl's place.

Looking back at poems I wrote before I was twenty-one, I'm startled because beneath the conscious craft are glimpses of the split I even then experienced between the girl who wrote poems, who defined herself in writing poems, and the girl who defined herself by her relationships with men.
—Adrienne Rich, poet

Mary Pipher, in her book, <u>Reviving Ophelia: Saving the Selves of Adolescent Girls</u>, describes the pressure of being young and female in the late twentieth century. She writes, "They are coming of age in a more dangerous, sexualized and media-saturated culture." In addition, adolescents themselves have responded with <u>Ophelia Speaks: Adolescent Girls Write about the Search for Self</u>. (These books and others are referenced in the Resources section.)

Cultural expectations and sex role stereotyping prevent some women from fulfilling their dreams of higher education and top-level careers. As we've already seen, many participants in my study were discouraged by parents, friends, and husbands. A disturbing comment came from Joan, who was working on her doctorate at the time of the study:

> *I lived all my life being told, "Yes, you're bright, but shut up. You talk too much." I was very clearly taught that in order to be a nice lady, you have to keep the lid on how bright you are.*

Some participants offered examples of gender role expectations. June, an engineer, described this experience during a high school awards assembly:

> *I was best in Math, and not as good in English. Some guy won the Math award, which I was hoping for. When the English award was given, I wasn't even listening, but I got it. I still feel like that was sexism.*

The problem of not being recognized for her math ability resurfaced when June went to see a University of Washington female counselor in 1981 about entering the relatively new department of Computer Science:

> *The counselor said I needed to take Calculus and such and such. I said, "That's okay, I don't have a problem with that. Math is my best area." She never would accept that. She kept saying I shouldn't try to get into the program. I said, "You don't understand; all the things you say I need to be good in, I <u>am</u> good in." What baffled me was, she didn't even hear it.*

Rachel, a teacher, tells what happened with a school counselor:

> *He wanted me to take Home Economics, but I refused. He got back at me. On*

Awards Day, he held onto a scholarship I had applied for, and instead of presenting it in front of the school assembly, he gave it to me the next day in the hall.

After graduation, the problem of not being taken seriously as a female can escalate. When two women in my study were ready to enter the job market, they found at least one profession still closed to females. At the time, gifted programs in America emphasized math and science, to keep up with Soviet schools in high technology. Brenda and Rachel decided on their own to become astronauts.

When Sputnik went up, they put me in Math Analysis and Physics and Chemistry and everything to groom me. But when I wanted to be an astronaut, I was told, "You can't apply." (Brenda)

I wanted to be an astronaut, too, and they said. "No, you can't do that." (Rachel)

Not only did these women receive little encouragement to succeed in so-called "careers for men," but they were told it simply wasn't possible. Kelly, a lawyer, and Carly, a physician, offered classic cultural stereotypes:

I still get people who are surprised I'm a lawyer. They ask me if I'm really a paralegal or a secretary. (Kelly)

If I ever told anyone I wanted to be a doctor, they said, "Oh, you want to be a nurse." I'd say, "No, I'm not interested in being a nurse." It took ten years before the culture shifted enough where at age 27 [1979], I started medical school, and people believed me. (Carly)

Once she got into medical school, though, sexism was still strongly present. Her group was astounded to hear that for Carly, the first question asked at the beginning of an oral medical exam was, "Why aren't you home having babies?"

Do you see how this country called Double Bind has made it difficult to be both bright and female? It is a cultural dilemma that we still face today. The following comment by Brenda is a powerful testament to the conflict involved in being a woman and being bright:

> *I was never told it was okay to be a girl.* <u>*My dad raised me like a boy, because I*</u> <u>*had intelligence.*</u> *For me, there was a loss of femininity, the whole side of me that made me a woman. Now I've had to go back over that part, telling myself it's okay to be a girl. That has made me stretch personally, and grow. (emphasis added)*

• • • • •

What messages about being female did you receive from parents, teachers and peers when you were growing up? How did you respond to these spoken and unspoken messages? How did they affect your self-confidence? How did they affect your career decisions and other life choices? (For a related chapter covering the positive side of this theme, see "Land of Remembering: Surviving on Strength.")

N O T E S

NOTES

4

LAND OF DUMBING DOWN:
"I played stupid, so nobody would know."

The third land, Dumbing Down, is closely related to the second one, Sexism. This concerns the inner conflict between being bright and female. Even though these women knew they were bright, they found it hard to celebrate it. In fact, many of the study participants hid their brightness, in order to fit in. The hiding of one's light was described by one woman in my study as "dumbing down."

For some of you, this might have happened when you were in school. If you got good grades, you said the teacher wasn't very hard, or you were just lucky. At work, if you got a promotion, you said the competition was light.

It almost seems normal to underestimate our abilities and achievements. This drives me crazy! I want you to let your light *shine,* not *hide it.*

For Brenda, "dumbing down" began in infancy, with her own baby book!

My mother told me that she had lied in my baby book, because people wouldn't believe some of the things that I did by myself. I had a vocabulary of over 100 words by the time I was one year old. She told me stuff like that all the time while I was growing up, but she didn't dare tell others.

Women have long bent to the cultural message that it is unfeminine to be bright. This is not just a problem from the history books. It's still happening today. According to recent studies, many women fear they will be rejected socially or be considered unfeminine if they appear to be too bright or too competent.

In a strange twist, many adolescent girls who are gifted actually use their intelligence to hide their abilities, so they can seem more attractive to adolescent boys. A study of adolescents pointed to "chameleon-like" behavior, where students either showed or hid their giftedness, depending on the reaction they expected from their peers.

Much courage is necessary for the decision in adolescence, if not before, to give up a bit of the present for the sake of the future; to ask, not only for the attention of men and boys, but also for the affirmation of one's inner sense of selfhood.

—Carolyn Heilbrun, in The Competent Woman

To fit in, many of the bright women in my study played the game of "dumbing down" throughout their school years:

Since fifth grade, I made sure I wasn't too good, too noticeable. (Diana)

In junior high, I wanted to fit in. I played stupid, so nobody would know that I was different. (Hope)

I had a tendency to slow down. I didn't want to finish assigned books in a week, so I just went with the flow. (Betty) [She spoke the last four words very slowly.]

I tried not to look different, not to look smart, not to be interested in things other people weren't interested in. (Mary)

In high school, and even through college, some of the women shrugged off their intelligence:

I never really considered myself smart; I just knew how to apply myself and studied. (Betty)

Some of my peers acknowledged that I was bright, but I just laughed that off. (Rose)

I did that [dumbing down] all the time, especially when I went away to college (June).

This chapter's theme concerns the double bind smart women face: they are expected to behave one way because they are smart, and another because they are women. On the one hand, they have the ability to be competent and bold; yet on the other, are taught it is inappropriate behavior to "brag" about one's successes or abilities. Too many women hide these accomplishments and traits in order not to alienate family, friends, or co-workers. They learn to "play it safe."

Or, we do it to ourselves when taking responsibility for our lives is too hard. Some women marry rather than face the anxiety of discovering whether they might reach their own goals and dreams. This is not a criticism of marriage—it's a criticism of the *reason* some women marry, which is to play it safe, to be protected.

A few women in my study hid their giftedness so completely that they could never acknowledge that trait, even to themselves, until adulthood.

I didn't own the term "gifted" for a long time, simply because it made me even more conspicuous. (Jill)

It wasn't until about the last four or five years that I finally accepted my gifted ness again, and my talents. (Rachel)

Even for the women in my study, dumbing down isn't just an experience of one's past. Roxanne and Brenda, for instance, spoke about it in very current terms:

There are still women who are very gifted but don't want to say anything, for fear of losing what they already have.   In a social gathering, I find myself chit-chatting about mundane things, which really is kind of negative. (Roxanne)

It's hard not to intimidate others with your brightness, but you almost sound patroniz ing by the time you're done trying to figure it out. (Brenda)

· · · · ·

Have you experienced a situation of "dumbing down" firsthand? Where were you when it happened? Who were you with at the time? In what situations are you likely to "dumb down," or deny your special gifts and talents? Where do you feel most encouraged to express your gifts and talents? (For a related chapter on the positive side of this theme, see "Land of Affirming: Smarting Up.")

NOTES

N O T E S

5

LAND OF NO CRACKS ALLOWED:
"Stay in control; never fail."

Even though the women in my study hid their intelligence at times, they still achieved academic success, especially in high school. Later in their lives, however, when success didn't come as easily, failure hit hard and deep. This is the fourth land in the country called Double Bind: No Cracks Allowed.

Because these women achieved easy, early academic success, dealing with failure later in their lives was not easy. For one woman, her "first inkling that things weren't always going to be smooth" came when she failed her first year of medical school. For another, "the first bad thing that had ever happened to me in my whole life, that first thing that I didn't get," was the unexpected death of her husband.

Asking for help in the hard times was not easy, and it was often misunderstood. Others seemed to expect these capable women to never need any help. Situations that were out of their control often threw them off balance. Control was an important issue for many of these women:

As long as I didn't lose control, I was okay. Things that I couldn't control took me for a loop more than anything else. (Roxanne)

I had always been able to handle everything, I had always been able to get what I wanted. Then I had this marriage going bad, and it was out of my control. It was hard at first to let go of the fact that I couldn't [steer] my life in the direction that I wanted it to go, after always being able to control it. (Ruth)

Shelly spoke of "this pattern of expecting you can handle anything":

When I was growing up, I was the one who kept things on an even keel. When my sister and father had a fight, I was the one who always tried to smooth it over. It's this pattern of expecting that you can handle anything that comes up, and that you can make everything right for yourself and everybody else. Then when you find out you can't, you don't have any mechanisms to deal with it.

Because they were unaccustomed to failing, they found it difficult to deal with failure when it did occur.

I still expect my life to go really well. I still am caught off guard when there's a hard part. (Diana)

I'm used to winning. When I run up against something where I'm not winning in other people's eyes, it's really hard to take. (Shelly)

Failing in one's own eyes is also difficult to handle.

For a long time I was a perfectionist, afraid of losing my edge, needing to continue to prove that I could achieve, being very afraid that I would fail. (Elaine)

Like a lot of you, I expect to be successful. So when I do something, I expect it to turn to gold in some way. When I hit the wall, I back off and internalize it as utter personal failure. While I generally have a very positive attitude towards myself, the pressure to do well usually comes from within. When I feel I'm an utter failure, I have to stop and say, "No, you're not." (Martha)

Added Joy, now a successful manager:

If I don't succeed the first time, it's a failure.

I relate so much to that quote! When I first began working as a consultant and college instructor, there were times when sessions went very well. In fact, that was the case most of the time. But there were a few times when they didn't. I felt like a failure. I would say to myself, "That's it. I'm done. I quit. I'm going to do something entirely different, like become a landscaper."

I eventually learned there is much room between success and failure, and I learned to give myself permission to not always be 100% excellent. I've even "grown up" enough to ask myself, "What can I learn from those times that don't go as well as I would have liked?"

Of course we want others to see us in a positive light, but remember that the burden of "no cracks allowed" is not a helpful one. We need to be willing to ask for help, and we need to understand that doing so is *not* a sign of weakness. Rather, some of the most competent people I know are those who understand when it's time to ask for help.

Joy explained to the group that though she feels self-reliant, there was a time when she really needed help and decided to ask her brother. She described the result as *a wonderful experience. Now we are close, because I finally turned to a sibling for help. I feel like we [women] need to reach out more than we do.*

The positive stereotype of these women shows them as bright, strong, capable, and competent. Unfortunately, family and friends find it hard to accept that a strong woman can feel weak. The following situations concern the negative side of this positive stereotype.

In my life, I'm the one who makes everything okay for other people. I'm the one who's in control, who problem-solves. The question is, When I need help, where do I go? Nobody knows how to nurture me, to help me. Because when I'm not in control, they all say, "Holy moley, where did that come from?" (Anne)

My sister called me when my father was in a coma, and I suddenly started to cry. My whole family thought I was having a breakdown. (Roxanne)

When I needed help everybody said, "Are you kidding? You're strong, you're confident, you're outgoing." (Brenda)

Martha summed up the situation when she said, "It sounds like most of us don't cave in easily, but when we do, people say, 'You can't do that. You can't cave in.'"

Comments from Diana point to a strong woman's dilemma of recognizing that she needs help, yet not knowing how to ask for it:

I never learned how to ask for help because I didn't have to ask for it all those years.

First you have to admit you're struggling, which you're not used to doing, and then you don't know how to ask. It makes it doubly hard.

In a sense, these women have internalized the problem of control and failure. They find it difficult to accept less than their best effort. They allow "no cracks," which is also part of their high self-expectations. One woman in the study told the group that she is currently president of one organization and will be state director of another the next year. But she brought laughter from the group when she added, "In my next life, I'd like to come back as a sheep."

• • • • •

Is No Cracks Allowed a land you have travelled to? What conflicts have you experienced in this land? What accomplishments are you proud of? When have you felt like a failure? What do you tell yourself in order to keep going? (For a related chapter on the positive side of this theme, see "Land of Acknowledging: All Goals Allowed.")

NOTES

6

MAY I SEE YOUR PASSPORT?

The socialization of women has been oriented toward virtue and acceptance, not toward power and competence, the double-bind impact of which has often been noted.
—*Rosalind Barnett and Grace Baruch,* The Competent Woman

Since we've wandered around for so long in the Country called Double Bind, are we doomed to live there forever? Of course not. It's a country many of us have to travel through, on our way to other lands.

There is a tale about a little boy who bragged to his mother that Tarzan conquered all of the jungle animals, even the mighty lion. The child's mother replied "My son, you will get a different story when the lion learns to write."

Like the lion, we women need to write our own stories, expressing our individual gifts to the world. We need to discover, speak and live our own truths.

One of the best ways to leave the country called Double Bind is to use the passport that each of us has been given. Our passport, in this case, is the parcel of gifts and talents that each of us owns. When we show this passport, we will be able to pass into the next country.

As women, we need to present this passport more than we've done in the past. We should not hide it or try to change it, just to please others. We can't let someone else tell us what our citizenship should be or where we should travel next.

We need to be the adventurous travelers we were meant to be, celebrating our packet of gifts and talents. When we show this passport at the border, we will be ready to pass into the country called Celebration.

A COUNTRY CALLED CELEBRATION

7

LAND OF ACHIEVING:
Dreams regained

More often than not, the women in my study criticized the usual connotations of the words <u>achievement</u> and <u>success</u>. Liz talked about having to change her own definition of achievement:

As a child, I was given a very limited concept of what achievement was. As an adult, my question is, 'How much achievement is enough?' I have very high self-expectations. Sometimes I ask myself, 'Is that really what life is about, producing this "stuff?" That's a mid-life question for me. The emphasis throughout my childhood on being bright, performing well, and producing good work in quantity has given me a lopsided view of what life is.

Two women presented a broader-than-normal definition of <u>achievement</u>. According to these women, achievement has little to do with money or education:

I will always have a concern to contribute to a better world. My other goals are to be creative to the full, to be expressive, and in everything to live, to love, to encounter people, to be present. I know that I'm successful at that and will be for the rest of my life. So I have achieved; I am achieving. (Elaine)

When you say achieve, I think of success, and when I think of success, I think of money. The person in my family making the most money is my brother the plumber. When I'm done, I'd like to be measured in terms of how I've touched people's lives. (Lynn)

Joan, a doctoral student, found herself in a double bind. On the one hand, she echoed the others, criticizing a limited view of achievement. But on the other hand, she admits she is still trying to achieve according to someone else's definition of the word:

Because I come from a gifted family and because I'm smart and all this stuff, even though I didn't perform well in college, [I keep thinking] a doctorate "must be what I need," and so I continue to push myself in directions that are not necessarily me.

Concluded Rose, a teacher of gifted children:

I've a feeling that the way we've defined success has been a barrier more than anything else. It makes us feel partly okay and partly [not okay, thinking,] "I should have done more."

Many in the group still feel guilty about not measuring up to high expectations from their childhood. Because of their high intelligence, they felt, as Rose said, that they "should have done more." Jill made a typical comment:

I feel guilty a lot. I've really had to struggle with the fact that I know I did not use my intelligence in a straight-line manner, to apply myself to learning.

Rose's view of achievement has changed for the better:

> *I'm feeling that I no longer have a drive to achieve. In high school, I wanted to <u>be</u> somebody, I wanted to <u>do</u> something significant. I think I'm finally getting to be happy with just being me.*

Some women, such as Penny, an educator and writer, commented on achievement in social terms:

> *I now realize I'm in the second half of my life and will do what I want to do, not what others want me to do. My greatest achievement: learning to [balance what I wanted to do with what others expected me to do.] That's not an achievement that you tack up on your wall, but it's a huge social achievement.*

The following comments from June, an engineer, illustrate the hollowness of certain kinds of achievement:

> *From a very young age, I knew there were three goals I wanted: a college degree, a beautiful home, and a husband. About four years ago, I achieved all those goals within one year of each other. All of a sudden my life stopped. About two years ago, I started spiralling into a deep depression, because I didn't have anything to look forward to. I've come out the other side, but I'm still searching for what I'm going to do in my adult life.*

These women struggled in a double bind, seeing achievement as "great accomplishments" and "outstanding careers," yet sensing internally that achievement ought to be more personal.

One of the greatest gifts the women in my study gave me was learning how important it is to really work on what achievement meant to me. I wanted to be in charge of my life, to be at the head of my parade, not dragging up the end! This search reminds me of the time in *Alice in Wonderland* when Alice asks the Cat which road she should take. The Cheshire Cat asks, "Where do you want to go?" Alice replies, "I don't really know." "Then," says the Cat, "it doesn't really matter which direction you go." Considering what achievement meant to me was like deciding which roads I wanted to take.

The cultural definition of success—moving up, having a bigger title, earning more money—is far too limiting. This can often leave us exhausted in body and spirit. Every time I brought up achievement with my study focus groups, the conversation immediately turned to what that work meant.

For my life, I've learned that achievement involves the "24-hour me," which means time for relaxation and play and exercise, plus my role as friend, wife and mother. This is similar to writing a personal mission statement, which Stephen Covey describes in his well-known book, <u>The 7 Habits of Highly Effective People.</u> When I worked on mine, my mission statement for my professional life included:

—to delight, challenge, and encourage women to celebrate their gifts and talents,

—to be a catalyst for enabling organizational members to work better together,

—to establish an educational learning environment that is emotionally safe, interesting, challenging, and exciting.

This helps me decide what I should and should not be doing, what fits, and what doesn't fit.

But I mentioned the 24-hour me, which includes:

—to be a loving and supportive wife,

—to be a fun and encouraging mother,

—to actively participate in promoting social justice in my community,

—to be an active member of my church,

—laugh, play, have fun.

This is what I mean by thinking about achievement in terms of the "24-hour you." For those of you who are at-home mothers, please remember that salary is *not* a requirement for defining achievement.

If we only see achievement as our professional work, then finding balance will be close to impossible. I've learned to feel very successful when I am able to spend a sunny afternoon in my yard and *not* feel guilty!

• • • • •

With what definitions of <u>achievement</u> and <u>success</u> did you grow up? How do you think the people around you today would define <u>achievement</u> and <u>success</u>? According to your own definitions of these words, what are you most proud of having achieved? In what ways have you succeeded in your life?

NOTES

8

LAND OF REMEMBERING:
Surviving on strength

Remembering who we were as children can bring us strength in adulthood. Most of the women in the study said it helped to remember their early days, even if those days were mostly painful. By having confidence in their own abilities, they were able to cope with pain, and that coping mechanism of self-confidence made them strong.

In her book, <u>The Girl Within</u>, Emily Hancock explores a woman's quest for her own identity by journeying back to her childhood:

> *At the buried core of women's identity is a distinct, vital self, first articulated in childhood, a root identity that gets cut off in the process of growing up. The women in my study came fully into their own and became truly themselves only when they recaptured the girl they'd been in the first place—before she got all cluttered up.*

Hancock's findings are remarkably similar to Carol Gilligan's, mentioned earlier. A preadolescent girl, according to Hancock, knows who she is and what she's about:

> *When she has the good fortune to grow up in a family that encourages her independence and applauds her achievements, a girl this age meets the world with confidence. Even*

if her circumstances are limited, a girl this age can aspire to far-reaching objecectives in her imagination—an inner realm no one else is privy to. There, if nowhere else, her ambitions are boundless, anything is possible.

She found that those women who could thread their way back to this girl from their past found in her a child to rely on and a source of womanly strength.

For the vast majority of the women in my own study, the "girl within" is bright and competent, as shown in the first land of Lost Dreams. Many of the women agreed that the memory of this childhood self was a source of strength. There is something about the "coreness" of childhood giftedness that extends into adulthood.

I really don't think I would be doing what I'm doing now if it weren't for knowing early on that I was bright and effective. (Joy)

It laid some groundwork that later I was able to come to, thank goodness, and re build. (Rachel)

It's been a ticket to a world not given me by my parents. (Mary)

It's just the sense that I'm good at something, and it doesn't matter what happens, because that [feeling of self-worth] remains. (Chris)

Three women in my study spoke about surviving hard times by holding on to an inner source of strength:

I've become a real survivor, and it's only because I know who I am that I can say,

'Now look, this has happened before, it will happen again, you can dust yourself off and keep going.' Having that kind of light inside, even though sometimes it doesn't come out, has been a real survival mechanism for me. (Brenda)

My first husband died when I had a little baby, and for a while it was really hard. I remember just instantly going into survival mode, saying, 'I've got to do this next, get a job,' and so forth. At one point, my mother said she really admired me for surviving. (A friend of hers, whose son was killed, had turned to the bottle.) Mom said, 'There were so many other things you could have done.' I just looked at her and asked, 'What else could I have done?' It's how you decide to approach life. You will survive, you will survive in style, and it all goes into that theme of who you are and how you face challenges. (Cindy)

I grew up in a crazy, abusive household. The thing that kept me sane was my outside success. I did a lot of self-talk: 'My house is crazy, but I'm not crazy.' When I grew up, people said, 'How can you do all those things: you're a marathon runner, grad student, working, with three kids, and keeping a 4.0 [GPA]. And I asked them, 'Well, what else could I do? There's no choice. That's what you do.' (Joy)

Later, Joy added:

I'm thankful that I was given brightness and effectiveness, because it's made me not only survive but flourish. I had to overcome quite a bit of adversity. I don't think I could have overcome that if I didn't, early on, have some real confidence in my abilities. Without that [confidence], I may have turned to alcohol or an easier way to deal with my issues in life.

Agreed Carrie:

> *I think my confidence in my abilities assisted me in saying, 'Okay, I'm going to work this through, and my own notion of my own success and giftedness will eventually bring me to the next step.'*

Remembering ourselves when we were competent young girls can make a difference in the way we move through our lives. When I was 11, 12 and 13, the ages when, according to studies, girls feel a strong sense of competence, I did feel capable and strong. I didn't shy from leadership; I moved right into it. I did well in school, and that sense of accomplishment followed me through my life. When we have that sense of confidence as young girls, we can continue to draw on that confidence in later years.

Though today's news often dwells on painful childhood memories from dysfunctional families, there is more to the past than pain. Many of the women in my study remembered that as bright young girls they felt a sense of happiness, even though heartache was also inevitable.

Perhaps having a difficult childhood makes us stronger as an adult, but it certainly is not a condition I would wish for anyone. I wish every young girl would come to understand that she is competent, she has many skills and abilities, and she is loved.

• • • • •

Have you discovered "a girl within" who is bright and able, the memory of which helps you now through difficult personal times? When cultural stereotyping pushes you to be less than you can be, how can you reach back to find strength from the girl you once were?

N O T E S

9

LAND OF AFFIRMING:
Smarting Up

As we've found, women experience a conflicting message: "Be bright, but don't show it." This is understandable, in light of cultural stereotypes of women. Even in today's movies, women are often portrayed as smart, witty and capable, but lose all sense of identity as soon as the leading man starts off on his own quest.

As women, we need to express our intelligence without apology. But how can we practice this "smarting up" when others encourage us to "dumb down"?

> *I ended up going to college, but I hadn't ever planned on it [until my high school counselor encouraged me to go.] My uncle had to sign papers, because my father refused to fund what he called "a husband hunt." I did not think I was gifted in any way. For a long time I thought, 'I am outspoken, and I have guts, but I'm not sure that makes me any brighter than anyone else.' But now I think that's a wonderful combination—to be bright, but to also have the confidence not to sit back and accept things that don't feel good. (Lynn)*

While these women were talking with one another in the group, they were able to say, without embarrassment, "I am intelligent."

I am not a victim, and I am not a puppet on somebody's string. Because I have an openness to life and to learning, I experience a lot very quickly. I guess for me it's been wonderful to be able to have the intelligence to see all points, all sides. (Rachel)

It seems paradoxical that these same women had trouble expressing their intelligence to others in their daily lives. Though they perceived giftedness as a core of their lives, they were sometimes hesitant to show it, because others did nothing to support it:

Being gifted has always been a sustaining force, though it wasn't recognized or supported by my family. I didn't have even a name for it. It was a core, maybe an invisible core. For me it's been a positive thread through good times and bad times. (Lucy)

Roberta said that men she knows are threatened by her intelligence:

I was always trying to find a man who could be my mate, who was intellectually a peer, a companion. I really like men. But having them be threatened by my brains makes me [jokingly say], "I'm sorry I'm smart, I can't help it!" I'm really not sorry, because having intelligence is such a source of strength and sustenance.

When society discourages women from showing their intelligence, two problems arise. Not only are women's abilities hidden, but *gifted women are literally hidden from one another.* When women in my study came together because of that common characteristic, each session was positive and uplifting.

When I was in college we had a fairly strong feminist group. Some of my dearest friends have come out of those groups, and this [gifted women's group] reminds me of that. We were given the space to be ourselves, and I very much miss that. It's a safe place where you can be who you are and give yourself credit for who you are. (Mary)

Other women made such comments as, "I can tell there are soulmates here," and "It's a wonderful thing to be able to sit with you and say, 'I'm really sharp,' and not feel like I'm hurting someone's feelings." When bright, competent women get together, they don't have to hide their talents and intelligence.

Gifted women need to start support groups of their own, to know they are not alone. There are groups of people who come together to say they are artists, not apologizing for being "only artists" or "part-time artists." Supportive groups for women would give them courage to acknowledge their special talents, not to bend to society's advice, "Be modest and not too bright." Thankfully, some school systems are doing this for gifted, pre-adolescent and adolescent girls.

A group of capable, supportive women could be far greater than the sum of its parts. A project that might be difficult for one person could be accomplished by the whole group. Many of the women in my study mentioned that they have always wanted to do something on an international scale for peace or world hunger. Perhaps a women's group could work together on a project they feel passionate about.

Lynn spoke eloquently about the need for "a new definition of genius, which is the compassionate genius":

For the last five years I've done extensive traveling internationally. It took until midlife for me to realize how most people on this planet live, to see what the real issues in life are. So I can sit here, separate, doing this heady kind of work, but my insides are torn with the total abject lifestyle and deprivation that are the norm for most people on this planet. So there is confusion in me about the value of emphasizing intellect, when I look at what the real needs of this world are.

I've belonged to a special support group I called an Empowerment Team, and our mission was to support one another in achieving our personal and professional goals. We rotated facilitating the meetings, which began with a quick check-in, followed by each member having time to ask the group for help or feedback or ideas. We might brainstorm a title to a training session, review something someone had written, or help with a decision that needed to be made.

The last step was for each of us to identify our goals for the next meeting, which could be anything we wanted—learning to sit quietly for ten minutes a day or writing something for work. This time in the meeting also included reporting on our progress— or non-progress!—on the goals we identified the previous meeting. It was quite motivating to tell the group what I planned to do, knowing they would be emailed to everyone, *plus* having to tell them at the next meeting whether or not they had been accomplished. I describe this part as holding each other "lovingly accountable." We did some marvelous work together. Consider beginning an Empowerment Team either at work or home. It helps so much to have the encouragement of others.

• • • • •

Do you belong to a supportive group of women with similar gifts and talents? If so, how can your group benefit from what you've read here? If not, what can you do to start a group in your area? With consistent, mutual support from a group of like-minded women, what achievements could emerge that would otherwise be stifled?

N O T E S

N O T E S

10

LAND OF ACKNOWLEDGING:
All Goals Allowed

As we've seen in the "No Cracks Allowed" chapter, women in my study found it difficult to handle failure. For these women, the positive stereotype of giftedness was that others thought of them as bright, capable, and competent. But it was difficult for family and friends to accept that these women also had times of normal vulnerability, times when they needed help.

Being labeled "gifted" encouraged academic success. These women took "Always Successful" as their motto. Unfortunately, when anything hard or unusual came along in life, they saw it as abnormal.

> *My feelings about the 'gifted' label are very mixed. I look at the word and I see a halo shimmering around with dark clouds at the edges. (Elaine)*

Strong, bright women often find it hard to accept less than their best effort. They view mediocrity as a loss of face. In Growing Up Gifted, Barbara Clark said, "Gifted women often believe they must excel in every role they play, and they must play in every role assigned." Comments by women in my study confirmed this:

Sometimes [being labeled 'gifted'] is positive and sometimes it's been a burden to live up to the expectations of being bright. On the whole, it's been positive, but there are times when I don't do the thing I really want to do because I'm <u>satisfying someone else's</u> <u>expectations</u>. I've made some of the transition toward satisfying my own expectations, but I probably haven't made it completely. (Chris, emphasis added)

A smart woman's double bind is, "The smarter you are, the more you are expected to accomplish. The more you don't achieve, the more you will seem to fail." But the question is, who sets up the barriers to achieving one's expectations? It may not always be history, culture or one's parents:

I think the barriers I have felt have been those I've erected for myself. (Rose)

Sue takes a practical, no-nonsense approach to goal-setting:

I've always done whatever I've wanted to do. Maybe that's bad, but if I have a goal, I work toward it. I did that as a kid, and I'm still doing it. I haven't achieved every thing I could, and I'm still working toward that.

Smart women often have a positive attitude about life—and a creative one. Lynn shared one of her favorite quotes with her group: "When your only tool is a hammer, you'll see every problem as a nail." Smart women learn to be creative, to have a diverse tool kit for solving their problems, including the belief that problems *can* be solved.

Joan told the group that though her goals are high, she looks forward to accomplishing them with joy:

I see life as a constant puzzle of adventure, unfolding. If life can be figured out, I'm going to be able to do it as well as anybody, the painful as well as the good parts.

As we've seen, the women in my study challenged our culture's definition of achievement, saying it wasn't broad enough. At times, they felt they <u>had</u> achieved, but it didn't count, because those achievements didn't fit the cultural definition of achievement.

This complaint echoed researchers' findings that the definition of achievement is highly biased. People choose the ways they will achieve according to the pressures they perceive about the variety of options they consider to be appropriate.

Based on this idea, were the women who dreamed of becoming doctors but instead became teachers, "underachievers?" Or, were they simply making a choice they considered "to be appropriate," taking into account society's discouragement of their higher career goals? Since teaching has long been considered an "appropriate" profession for women, it follows that teaching should be seen as a great achievement, not an underachievement.

We need to consider female achievement as <u>more than</u> professional success, and as <u>different from</u> society's standards of ideal achievement. Society's message for women has long been, "Lower your sights. Express your goals not in large world affairs, but within the family and community." From this perspective, "appropriate" can be seen as underachievement.

Other studies conclude that when it comes to achievement, women cite interpersonal relationships or emotional well-being. This is similar to Daniel Goldman's important book, <u>Emotional Intelligence</u>. The hallmarks of emotional intelligence are knowing your own feelings, as well as others,' and being able to handle those feelings skillfully. Abilities such as empathy, self-awareness, and managing anxiety are important. Intelligence then becomes only a *part* of achievement and success.

A key factor for outward achievement is what gifted females <u>believe</u> they can attain or accomplish professionally. Sue said that the gifted label helped, but it wasn't necessary in achieving what she wanted in life:

> *The label of being gifted was a sort of confirmation, but it wasn't the central thing: <u>what you feel capable of doing.</u> It's really a more personal thing than it is an IQ thing. (emphasis added)*

Believing that one can—and is entitled to—attain high professional achievements is hard for many capable women to do. Here is where gifted women come up against the double bind of being expected to behave one way because they are gifted—that is, to achieve—and another way because they are women—to support and nurture others.

Traditional models of achievement can't remain the standard for everyone. A woman's motivations to achieve can often be vastly different from a man's. Whereas traditionally we'd expect everyone to want to "get ahead," *not* electing to engage in some activity or promotion may reflect an alternative choice rather than avoidance.

A woman, in other words, may choose to live a comparatively quiet life as a research scientist rather than to step into the limelight as an astronaut. To others, she may not have achieved much in terms of recognition and material success. But in her own mind, she has chosen a career that gives her great personal satisfaction.

We need to affirm women's choices, while still acknowledging the messages of history and culture that helped to shape these choices. Instead of asking the question, "Why aren't women more like men?" we need to ask, "Why do people make the choices they do?"

Asking that question affirms the choices of both men and women, allowing us to encourage one another's goals.

There is a word that describes the women in my study: "omnipotentiality," meaning "having many talents." Instead of saying that a smart woman is scatter-brained because she finds it hard to choose among various life options, it's better to say she has omnipotentiality. The difficulty lies in knowing that when she chooses one talent or gift, she has to let go of others, at least for a time.

Consider finding "balcony people" to help you make those choices. Balcony people are the people in my life who stand on that metaphorical balcony and cheer, "Go, Alice, go! You can do it. We believe in you." I need all the balcony people I can find! I don't need "basement people, " who say, "Come on down here where it's dark, and we can moan and complain about what's the matter with everyone else." Balcony people encourage us and help us believe in ourselves.

As a bright, capable woman, view your life goals according to your gifts and talents. Take steps toward those goals, knowing you are making your own choices, not making decisions based on outside pressures. Don't hide them; don't be talked out of them. Let your light shine. In this way, you can live in the country of Celebration.

Where have all the smart women gone? Look in your mirror!

• • • • •

What is one main life goal of yours? Are you on the road toward accomplishing that goal? If not, when did you last believe that you were on that road? How far away is that goal? What steps will you take to reach it?

NOTES

NOTES

N O T E S

AFTERWORD

Mom's Last Room

My Ph.D. dissertation was completed several years ago. There have been many changes for women since then. Hopefully, no one today asks why a woman studying to be a doctor isn't home having babies. Today there are lots of female role models for younger women to emulate. Women have successfully entered many male-dominated professions, plus many have become entrepreneurs and run their own businesses. And others have intentionally said goodbye to their success in the corporate world to stay home with their children. With the help of technology, many can have at-home businesses.

But some things have not changed. Girls are still bombarded with messages about how they should look and how they should behave. It seems that 8 year-olds become teenagers way before their 13th birthday. A Country called Double Bind still exists. The work world remains largely unchanged, with two weeks for vacation and 40-hour weeks. Private and public enterprises have not changed enough to acknowledge that most workers are working *parents*.

It's not fair to put the burden on women, to figure out how to combine career and family. That's not where the change needs to happen. It needs to happen in the work place. We need far more part-time and shared jobs that give equitable benefits. So many women, caught between the choice of 0 hours or 40 hours, know they can't afford 0, but don't need 40. I believe there are many mothers *and* fathers who would be willing to work less hours when their children are young.

My own mother worked full time when I was young, and I think she would have happily chosen a shared or equitable part-time job rather than full time.

My wonderful mother-in-law was a hard-working mom, too. Now she is near the end of her life. Where she is living now will be her last room. It is just a studio apartment, small but cozy. Around her on every wall and even the back of her door are pictures--pictures of each of her children on their wedding day, pictures of her grandchildren, her deceased husband, friends. Every picture is about people. Every picture is about love.

What are those things that, when your life is coming to a close, will remain on your walls?

I'll want to see some of the same kind of pictures as Mom: graduations, weddings, special moments from trips, the kids, maybe grand kids. Pictures of love. Then I think I'd like to see my diplomas, plus some of my favorite art. And if there isn't natural beauty out my window, I'll need some more photos.

What pictures will you have on your walls?

The truth is, right now each of us is living in our last room. We can't take a picture without focus. We can't focus unless we are free from fear. We need to be supported by our balcony people, we need to understand what achievement means, we need to feel bold enough to make the choices we want, not what others might expect. We must see clearly our heart's desire and our mind's passions.

Imagine buying frames. What will be in them? It's your room, your life.

RESOURCES

BOOKS

Adams, Caroline Joy. <u>A Woman of Wisdom: Honoring and Celebrating Who You Are</u>, Celestial Arts, 1999.

Belenky, et al. <u>Women's Ways of Knowing: the Development of Self, Voice, and Mind</u>, Basic Books, 1986.

Billington, Dottie. <u>Life is an Attitude: How to Grow Forever Better</u>, Lowell Leigh Books, 2000.

Brown, Genevieve and Irby, Beverly, eds. <u>Women and Leadership: Creating Balance in Life</u>, Nova Science,1998.

Clark, Barbara, <u>Growing Up Gifted</u>, 5th edition, Charles E. Merrill, 1997.

Colangelo and Davis, ed. <u>Handbook of Gifted Education</u>, Allyn Press, 1996.

Gilligan, Carol. <u>In a Different Voice: Psychological Theory and Women's Developent,</u> Harvard University Press, reissued edition, 1993.

Hancock, Emily, <u>The Girl Within,</u> E.P. Dutton, 1989.

Heilbrun, Carolyn. <u>Writing a Woman's Life</u>, Ballentine, 1988.

Kerr, Barbara. <u>Smart Girls: A New Psychology of Girls, Women and Giftedness (Smart Girls Two)</u>, Gifted Psychology Press, 1997.

Noble, Kathleen, <u>The Sound of the Silver Horn: Reclaiming the Heroism in Contemporary Women's Lives</u>, Fawcett Columbine,1994.

Odean, Kathleen. <u>Great Books for Girls: More than 600 Books to Inspire Today's Girls and Tomorrow's Women</u>, Ballentine Pub. Group, 1997.

Orenstein, Peggy. <u>Flux: Women on Sex, Work, Kids, Love and Life in a Half-changed World</u>, Doubleday, 2000.

Pipher, Mary. <u>Reviving Ophelia: Saving the Selves of Adolescent Girls</u>, Random House, 1994.

Reis, Sally. <u>Work Left Undone: Choices and Compromises of Talented Women</u>, Creative Learning, 1998.

Rimm, Sylvia. <u>See Jane Win: The Rimm Report on How 1,000 Girls Became Successful</u>, Three Rivers Press, 1999.

Shandler, Sara. <u>Ophelia Speaks: Adolescent Girls Write about their Search for Self</u>, Harper Collins, 1999.

Snyderman, Nancy. <u>Necessary Journeys: Letting Ourselves Learn from Life</u>, Hyperion, 2000.

Walker, Betty and Marilyn Mehr. <u>The Courage to Achieve: Why America's Brightest Women Struggle to Fulfill their Promise</u>, Simon & Schuster, 1992.

WEB PAGES

WOMEN

Bizwomen.com
>   On-line interactive community for business women.

Electrapages.com
>   Directory of women's businesses and organizations.

Expage.com/page/giftedwomen
>   Books, articles, references about gifted women.

Talentdevelop.com
>   Collection of articles, interviews, etc. related to giftedness and creative expression.

Womenconnect.com
>   News relating to women, plus library with many topics.

Wwwomen.com
>   Directory of women's web sites.

GIRLS

Girlsinc.org
>   Inspiring girls to be strong, smart, and bold.

GIFTED EDUCATION

www.nagc.org

National Association of Gifted Education. NAGC "is an organization of parents, educators, other professionals and community leaders who unite to address the unique needs of children and youth with demonstrated gifts and talents as well as those children who may be able to develop their talent potential with appropriate educational experiences."

AT-HOME MOTHERS

Here are some Internet sites that provide more information for and about at-home mothers.

www.AtHomeMothers.com
www.MochaMoms.org
www.Momsnetwork.com
www.Hearts-At-Home.org
www.Momsclub.org

WOMEN'S ORGANIZATIONS AND ASSOCIATIONS

All of these groups have the advancement and support of women in mind. There are likely many of these in your community. Consider joining one. The mission statements and other information in quotes come directly from their web pages, and hopefully gives you an idea about which one(s) might be a good match for you.

American Association of University Women
>www.aauw.org
>800-326-2289
>1111 16th St. NW
>Washington, D.C. 20036

The AAUW "promotes equity for all women and girls, lifelong education, and positive societal change."
>Canadian Federation of University Women (same as AAUW)

American Business Women's Association
>www.abwa.org
>800-228-0007
>P.O. Box 8728
>Kansas City, MO 64114

Their mission is "to bring together businesswomen of diverse occupations and to provide opportunities for them to help themselves and others grow personally and professionally through leadership, education, networking support, and national recognition."

American Nurses Association

www.ana.org
800-274-4262
600 Maryland Ave, SW Suite 100
Washington, D.C. 20024

"The ANA advances the nursing profession by fostering high standards of nursing practice, promoting the economic and general welfare of nurses in the workplace."

Association for Women in Communications

www.womcom.org
410-544-7442
780 Ritchie Hwy, St 285
Servanna Park, MD 21146

Their mission is "a professional organization that champions the advancement of women across all communications disciplines by recognizing excellence, promoting leadership and positioning its members at the front of the evolving communications era."

Association for Women in Computing

www.awc-hq.org
415-905-4663
41 Sutter St. Suite 1006
San Francisco, CA 94104

AWC "is a national, nonprofit, professional organizaton for individuals with an interest in information technology."

American Society of Women Accountants
www.aswa.org
800-326-2163
1595 Spring Hill Rd. Suite 330
Vienna, VA 22182
"The mission of ASWA is to enable women in all accounting and related fields to achieve their full personal, professional and economic potential and to contribute to the future development of their profession."

Business and Professional Women
www.bpwusa.org
202-293-1100
2012 Mass. Ave NW
Washington, D.C. 20036
BPW "promotes equity and economic self-sufficiency for all women through advocacy, education and information." The national focus is on legislative issues, and local levels focus on professional skill development in addition to the legislative platform.

International Association of Administrative Professionals
www.iaap-hq.org
816-891-6600
P.O. Box 20404
Kansas City, MO 64195
An association for administrative support staff, they "provide up-to-date research on office trends, cutting-edge publications, outstanding seminars and conferences, and top-notch resources to help administrative professionals enhance their skills."

League of Women Voters
    www.lwv.org
    202-429-1965
    1730 M St.. NW Suite 1000
    Washington, D.C. 20036
"The LWV, a nonpartisan political organization, encourages the informed and active participation of citizens in government, works to increase understanding of major public policy issues, and influences public policy through education and advocacy."

National Association of Female Executives
    www.nafe.com
    800-634-6233
    P.O. Box 469031
    Escondido, CA 92046
"NAFE provides resources and services--through education, networkng, and public advocacy--to empower its members to achieve career success and financial security."

National Association of Women Business Owners
    www.nawbo.org
    800-556-2926
    1411 K St. NW, Suite 1300
    Washington, D.C. 20005
NAWBO assists women business owners to "find support and resources to help you grow your business and enrich your life."

National Association for Women's Health
www.nawh.org
312-786-1468
300 W. Adams St. Suite 328
Chicago, IL 60606
NAWH is "dedicated to improving the quality of women's health by integrating the best of business, science, policy and clinical practice."

National Partnership for Women and Families
www.nationalpartnership.org
202-986-2600
1875 Connecticut Ave. NW suite 710
Washington, D.C. 20009
This nonprofit organization "uses public education and advocacy to promote fairness in the workplace, quality health care, and policies that help women and men meet the dual demands of work and family."

Soroptimist International
www.siahq.com
800-942-4629
Two Penn Center Plaza Suite 1000
Philadelphia, PA 19102
This is "a volunteer service organization for women in business, management and the professions" and the heart of their mission is to "make a difference for women" through volunteer service to the community.

YWCA

www.ywca.org
212-465-2281
Empire State Bldg
350 5th Ave. Suite 301
New York, NY 10118

The YWCA "draws together members who strive to create opportunities for women's growth, leadership and power in order to attain a common vision: peace, justice, freedom and dignity of all people."

Zonta International

www.zonta.org
312-930-5848
557 W. Randolph St.
Chicago, IL 60661

Zonta "supports international service projects and educational fellowships to improve the quality of life for women." Individual Zonta clubs select, fund and participate in community projects which address issues such as women's economic self-sufficiency, legal equality, access to education and health, and eradicating violence."

ADDITIONAL RESOURCES

If you are considering beginning college or returning to college, there are programs that can be helpful to you:

Women's Centers

Found on most college campuses, women's centers have programs and speakers, plus often offer advising for women.

Displaced Homemakers

Many community colleges offer this program. It is a great place to ease into college and explore life options. Eligibility is based on re-entering the labor market on a full-time basis due to divorce, widowhood, or disability of spouse. Program participants learn how to prepare to enter the labor market, or to enter school as a step towards employment.

ORDER FORM

QTY.	Price	CAN. Price	Total
	$12.95	$19.95	
Shipping and Handling (add $2.50 for one book, $1.00 for each additional book)			
Sales tax (WA residents only, add 8.2%)			
Total Enclosed			

Fax orders: 360-650-1031. Send this form.
Online orders: SPBooks@premier1.net or www.alicerowe.com
Postal orders: Smart People Books, 149 Sudden Valley, Bellingham, WA 98226

Payment: Please Check One
❑ Check
❑ VISA
❑ MasterCard

Expiration Date: _____/_____
Card #: _____
Name on Card: _____

Name _____
Address _____
City _____ State _____ Zip _____
Daytime Phone (   ) _____
Email Address _____

Please send FREE information on Alice Rowe's:
❑ management keynotes/seminars ❑ women's issues-keynotes/seminars

Quantity discounts are available.

ABOUT THE AUTHOR

Dr. Alice Rowe creates and delivers training programs for business, industry, government, and the professions. She provides tools for enabling clients to increase performance by developing strong management skills and building effective teams. Her innovative and enthusiastic presentation style has generated a high demand for her services. Dr. Rowe also facilitates retreats and meetings, helping the group stay focused and energized.

A unique blend of corporate trainer, educator, and public speaker, Alice Rowe has worked in her profession for over twenty years and has consulted with over 100 diverse organizations. As an educator, she has taught on the community, college, and masters level.

This book is a reflection of Dr. Rowe's deep interest in women's issues. She continues this interest by frequently presenting dynamic keynote speeches and workshops. Participants appreciate her warmth, her genuine concern for people, and her humor. If you are intersted in working with her, contact her at

www.alicerowe.com
arowe@premier1.net.
149 Sudden Valley
Bellingham, WA 98226